Copy Right

For permissions requests, contact the publisher at
epic.verity@gmail.com

Content

Intoduction

Meet the tech genius who turned a childhood love for computers into a worldwide revolution! Dive into the fascinating life of Bill Gates, the brilliant mind behind the magic of Microsoft.

From a curious kid in Seattle to the billionaire genius who dreamed of a computer on every desk, this biography is a journey through the exciting world of innovation. Get ready to discover how a teenager's passion for coding paved the way for the digital age we live in today.

Bill Gates isn't just a tech guru; he's a real-life superhero of the computer world, and his story is nothing short of extraordinary!

4

Chapter 1
A Curious Kid

Once upon a time, back in 1955, there was a boy named Bill Gates. But this wasn't just any ordinary kid - Bill was super curious and smart. He was born in Seattle, Washington, a place known for its rainy days and coffee shops. From a young age, Bill had this incredible desire to explore and learn about all sorts of new things.

Picture a little Bill, with big glasses and a grin that showed how much he loved figuring out the world around him. His curiosity was like a little flame inside him, always burning with questions and ideas.

In the cozy city of Seattle, where raindrops played a musical tune on the rooftops, young Bill found joy in discovering the secrets of the universe. Whether it was how birds could fly or

why the sky changed colours, he was always on a mission to unlock the mysteries of life.

As he grew older, this curiosity led him to a world that was just starting to see the light of computers. Bill was fascinated by these magical machines that could do incredible things. Little did he know, this fascination would spark a journey that would change the world of technology forever.

So, imagine a rainy afternoon in Seattle, with young Bill hunched over a mysterious box of wires and buttons, his eyes gleaming with the excitement of a new adventure. Little did he know that his journey was just beginning, and the world was about to witness the rise of a curious kid who would shape the future in ways no one could have imagined.

Chapter 2
Computer Love

As the 1960s dawned, a teenage Bill Gates found himself enchanted by a new fascination—computers. Imagine a world where computers were not sleek and shiny gadgets but colossal machines with blinking lights and mysterious buttons. It was during this time that Bill, with his insatiable curiosity, discovered his love for these magical devices.

At his school in Seattle, Bill stumbled upon a place that would become his second home—the computer center. This wasn't just any computer; it was a massive, hulking machine that required special rooms to house its electronic brain. The air buzzed with excitement as Bill delved into the world of coding and programming.

Picture a young Bill, glasses perched on his nose, furrowing his brow in concentration as he tapped away at the keys. In those moments, he wasn't just typing random characters; he was crafting the future. Each line of code was like a stroke of a painter's brush, creating a masterpiece in the digital realm.

With each passing day, Bill's passion for computers grew. He wasn't content with just using them; he wanted to understand how they worked, to unravel the secrets hidden within their electronic circuits. It wasn't long before he became a regular at the computer center, spending hours exploring the vast possibilities that these machines offered.

His teenage years were marked by a unique blend of school, friends, and an ever-growing fascination with the potential of computers. The world was changing, and young Bill Gates was right there at the forefront, eagerly embracing the digital wave that was about to reshape the course of history.

Little did he know that this love for computers was just the beginning. The seed of passion planted in those early years would soon sprout into something extraordinary, setting the stage for the incredible journey that lay ahead.

Chapter 3
First Venture

Now, imagine a time when bell-bottoms were in style, and disco balls were a thing. In the midst of the funky 1970s, our teenage computer whiz, Bill Gates, took his passion to the next level. At the young age of 13, he joined forces with his friend Paul Allen to embark on an exciting journey—they started their first business, the Lakeside Programmers Club.

The Lakeside Programmers Club wasn't your typical after-school activity. It was a cool and daring venture fueled by Bill and Paul's love for computers. Picture them huddled over their machines, surrounded by the hum of computer processors and the glow of screens.

These two friends weren't just dreaming of the future; they were crafting it, one line of code at a time.

Their business wasn't about selling lemonade or mowing lawns. No, it was about something much more cutting-edge—computers. Bill and Paul were on a mission to turn their shared passion into something bigger, something that could make a mark on the world.

The Lakeside Programmers Club wasn't an overnight success. It was a journey filled with challenges and triumphs, a journey that shaped the entrepreneurial spirit of a young Bill Gates. They weren't just programming for fun; they were laying the groundwork for what would become a tech revolution.

As the Lakeside Programmers Club took its first steps, Bill and Paul were learning valuable lessons about teamwork, business, and the limitless possibilities of the digital world. Little did they know that this was just the beginning of a series of adventures that would lead them to the forefront of the technology revolution, transforming their teenage dreams into the powerhouse

that would eventually be known as Microsoft. The Lakeside Programmers Club wasn't just a small start-up; it was the spark that ignited a blazing trail toward the future.

Chapter 4
Harvard Days

Now, let's fast forward to a time when disco music was grooving, and bell-bottom pants were the fashion. Bill Gates, the same curious kid who once explored the wonders of computers in his teenage years, found himself at Harvard University in the 1970s. Harvard was no ordinary school; it was a prestigious place filled with ancient brick buildings, towering libraries, and an atmosphere buzzing with intellect.

Bill, with his love for computers burning bright, joined the halls of Harvard. But here's the twist: he didn't stick around for the typical four-year college journey. Nope, Bill Gates had bigger dreams bubbling inside him, dreams that involved making computers accessible to everyone.

In 1975, Bill decided to take a bold step. He dropped out of Harvard, leaving behind the traditional college life to follow his passion. Why? Because he believed in a future where computers wouldn't just be for the elite few but for everyone, from Seattle to Singapore.

Now, picture this: Bill, with his wild curly hair and determined eyes, teamed up once again with his friend Paul Allen. Together, they set out to change the world. They founded a little company called Microsoft, a name that would soon become synonymous with personal computers.

At Microsoft, they weren't just playing around with fancy gadgets. Bill and Paul were creating software that would form the foundation for the computers we use every day. It was like building the magical spells that brought computers to life.

Their first big breakthrough was MS-DOS, an operating system that became the heart and soul of IBM's first personal computer. Suddenly, computers weren't just giant machines in university basements; they were becoming a part of everyday life.

But the story doesn't stop there. In the 1980s, Microsoft introduced something that would revolutionize the way we interact with computers—Windows. It wasn't just an operating system; it was like adding a friendly face to the world of technology. People could now click, drag, and drop instead of typing complicated commands. Bill's dream of a computer on every desk and in every home was slowly turning into reality.

And guess what? By the time Bill Gates was 31, he became a billionaire. That's like being the coolest genius in the tech world. But here's the thing about Bill—he wasn't content with just having a mountain of gold. He and his then-wife Melinda started the Bill & Melinda Gates Foundation in 1994, using their wealth to tackle big problems like poverty and diseases around the globe.

So, there you have it—Bill Gates, the college dropout who became a genius of computers and a superhero for the world. Stay tuned for more adventures in the ever-evolving saga of this tech trailblazer!

Chapter 5
The Birth of Microsoft

Alright, grab your time-travelling goggles because we're zooming back to the cool '70s. Remember Bill Gates, the computer whiz with dreams bigger than the moon? Well, after leaving Harvard in 1975, Bill and his buddy Paul Allen embarked on an epic journey that changed the face of technology forever.

This is where the story of Microsoft begins. In a world where personal computers were like rare treasures guarded by dragons, Bill had a vision - a wild dream of having a computer in every home, on every desk. It was like turning magic into reality, and so, Microsoft was born.

Bill and Paul, with their brains buzzing like busy bees, started creating

software. But not just any software - the kind that would be the heartbeat of personal computers. They weren't just coding; they were building the very building blocks of the digital world we live in today.

Their first big hit? MS-DOS! It sounds like a secret code, doesn't it? Well, it kind of was! MS-DOS became the magical spell that made IBM's first personal computer come alive. Now, imagine a world where you needed to speak the language of computers to make them do things. MS-DOS was like a magical translator, making computers understand us regular folks without needing a degree in computer genius.

But the adventure didn't stop there. In the '80s, Microsoft unleashed something that would make computers not just smart but friendly too - Windows. Picture this: a colourful interface with icons and buttons, a world where you could click and drag instead of typing away like a robot. It was like adding a dash of magic to the tech world, making computers feel like your friend rather than a mysterious machine.

Guess what happened next? Bill Gates, our computer genius, became a billionaire in 1987 at the tender age of 31. It was like reaching the highest level in a video game, but instead of a game, it was real life!

But hold on tight; the adventure is just getting started. In the chapters to come, you'll discover how Microsoft shaped the internet age, faced challenges, and how Bill Gates, the billionaire with a heart of gold, turned into a real-life superhero. So, young adventurer, get ready for more twists and turns in this epic tale of tech, dreams, and the birth of Microsoft!

Chapter 6
DOS Days

Alright, young adventurer, imagine a world where computers spoke a secret language, and only a few genius could understand it. Well, Bill Gates, our tech hero, wasn't satisfied with that. He wanted to make computers friendly and easy for everyone to use.

So, in the DOS days of the 1980s, Microsoft, the company Bill co-founded, created something magical—MS-DOS. Hold on, what's MS-DOS? Think of it as a magical spell book that translated our everyday words into the language that computers could understand.

With MS-DOS, you didn't need to be a computer genius; you could simply tell your computer what to do, like casting a spell with words.

Now, picture this: IBM, a giant in the tech world, was creating its first personal computer. But what good is a computer without an operating system, right? That's where MS-DOS came to the rescue! It became the brain, the heart, and the soul of IBM's computer. It was like teaching a powerful dragon to dance to our tune.

Thanks to MS-DOS, computers were no longer mysterious and intimidating; they were becoming our helpful companions. People could now type commands, and the computer would respond, opening up a whole new world of possibilities. It was a game-changer, and Bill Gates was at the forefront of this revolution.

But hold on tight, because the adventure doesn't end there. As technology continued to evolve, Bill and his team at Microsoft were cooking up something even more enchanting—Windows! Picture a colourful world where you didn't have to type commands; you could simply click, drag, and drop. Windows, with its graphical interface, made computers as easy to use as playing your favourite video game.

With MS-DOS and Windows, Bill Gates was turning his dream into reality. A computer on every desk and in every home was not just a dream anymore; it was happening. The world was entering a new era of technology, and Bill Gates was leading the charge.

So, dear adventurer, in the next chapters, you'll witness how Microsoft shaped the internet age, faced challenges, and see how Bill Gates, the tech genius, transformed into a real-life superhero. Get ready for more magic and innovation in the upcoming chapters of this incredible tale!

Chapter 7
Windows Revolution

Imagine a world where computers weren't just boxes of mystery but friends that understood you with a click and a colourful interface. Welcome to the magical realm of Windows, where the computer became more than a tool; it became a friendly companion, thanks to the genius mind of Bill Gates.

In the enchanting 1980s, Microsoft introduced Windows, an operating system that transformed the way we interacted with computers.

Before, it was like talking to a robot using secret codes (remember DOS?). But now, with Windows, it was like having a conversation with a friend who understood pictures and colours.

Windows made computers user-friendly.

Instead of typing complex commands, you could click on icons, and windows would open, revealing a world of possibilities. Imagine having a magical door that led to different rooms of your castle, each filled with wonders and adventures. That's what Windows did for computers.

This revolutionary operating system had colourful icons and a mouse that allowed you to navigate seamlessly. It was like conducting a symphony of technology with a wave of your hand. You could write stories, create art, and even play games - all at the click of a mouse.

With Windows, computers became accessible to everyone. It wasn't just for tech geniuses; it was for kids, grandparents, and everyone in between. Bill Gates' dream of a computer on every desk and in every home was one step closer to reality.

The Windows revolution wasn't just about making technology fun; it was about making it a tool for creativity and learning. Imagine painting a digital masterpiece or writing a novel without the hassle of complex commands.

Thanks to Windows, these dreams became a colourful reality.

So, young adventurers, as we step into the Windows era, remember that it's not just about technology; it's about creating a world where everyone can be a part of the magic. Get ready for more tales of innovation, challenges, and the incredible journey of our tech hero, Bill Gates!

Chapter 8
The Billionaire

In the magical world of technology, where computers transformed into friendly companions and dreams took the shape of software, Bill Gates reached a milestone - the Billionaire's Summit. At the young age of 31, our tech hero found himself at the peak of success, surrounded by a vast kingdom of ones and zeros.

Becoming a billionaire meant that Bill's dream of a computer on every desk and in every home was turning into reality.

His vision had taken flight, and the world was witnessing the power of ideas and innovation. Imagine having a treasure chest filled not with gold coins but with the endless possibilities of technology.

Bill Gates' journey from a curious kid to a computer genius had brought him to a place where he could make a difference on a global scale. The billions were not just a symbol of wealth; they were a key to unlocking doors that led to solutions for some of the world's most significant challenges.

But with great power come great responsibility. Bill, along with his then-wife Melinda, recognized that the treasure they had amassed could be used to change lives. It was time to embark on a new quest, one that involved giving back to the world and making it a better place.

And so, the Gates Foundation was born. This charity organisation aimed to use their wealth not just for personal gain but to tackle global issues like poverty and disease. It was a noble mission, turning the billionaire's story into a tale of compassion and social impact.

Young minds, let this chapter be a beacon of inspiration. Becoming a billionaire wasn't the end of the story for Bill Gates; it was a beginning, a chance to rewrite the narrative of success.

As we delve deeper into the enchanted chapters ahead, witness how the power of giving transforms our tech hero into a philanthropic genius, shaping the world for the better.

Chapter 9
Philanthropy Begins

As the story of Bill Gates unfolded, a new chapter began - one filled with compassion, empathy, and a deep desire to make the world a better place. In the enchanted year of 1994, Bill and his then-wife Melinda embarked on a magical journey to start the Bill & Melinda Gates Foundation.

The foundation was not a castle made of stone and gold but a stronghold of hope and goodwill. Bill and Melinda, armed with their wealth and a genuine wish to help others, set out to tackle global challenges like poverty and disease.

It was as if they held a wand that could cast spells to heal the world.

Imagine a world where every child could go to school, where diseases like malaria and polio were mere fairy tales of the past. This was the dream that Bill and Melinda nurtured within the walls of their foundation. Their treasure trove was not just riches; it was a force for good, a beacon that could light up even the darkest corners of the earth.

With a wave of philanthropic magic, the Gates Foundation became one of the world's largest private charitable foundations. It focused on health, education, and poverty alleviation on a global scale, spreading its wings far and wide. It wasn't about the number of zeros in their bank account but the impact those zeros could make in the lives of others.

Bill Gates, once a computer genius, now turned into a philanthropic sorcerer, casting spells of change and hope. The foundation's initiatives were like scrolls of wisdom, providing education to those who lacked it,

offering healthcare to the sick, and striving to eradicate the shadows of poverty.

Dear reader, let this chapter be a reminder that magic isn't just in fairy tales; it's in the deeds of those who choose to make a difference. As we journey through the enchanted pages ahead, witness how Bill Gates, armed with kindness and generosity, continues to shape a world where everyone has a chance for a brighter tomorrow.

Chapter 10
Internet Explorer and the Internet Age

Dear adventurer, it's time to embark on a thrilling journey into the world of the Internet, where Bill Gates, the tech genius, played a pivotal role in shaping the landscape of the digital realm. Picture this - it's the late 20th century, and the Internet is like a vast, uncharted territory waiting to be explored.

As the 1990s unfolded, Bill Gates and his team at Microsoft introduced a magical gateway known as Internet Explorer. Think of it as the key that opened the door to the World Wide Web for millions around the globe. Internet Explorer wasn't just a browser;

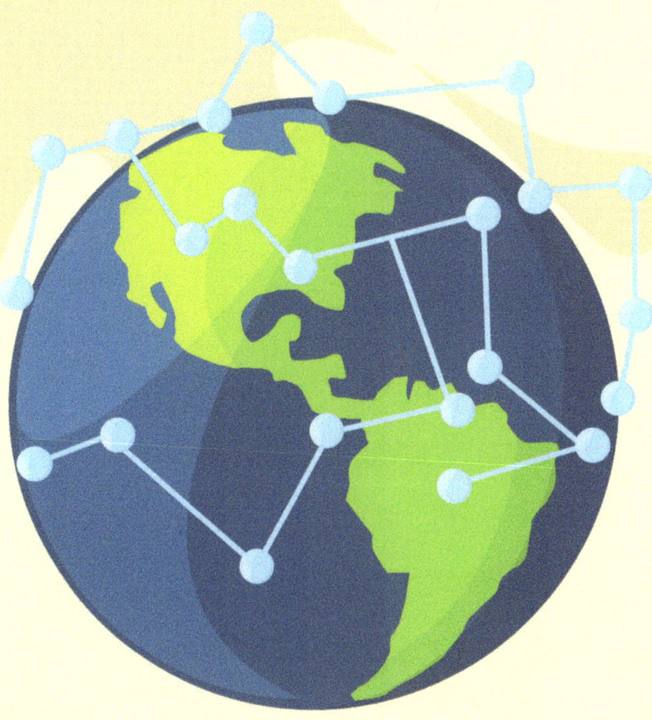

it was a window to a new era, an age where information, communication, and endless possibilities were at your fingertips.

Picture young minds like yours discovering the wonders of the Internet – a place where you could learn, connect, and explore like never before. Internet Explorer became the enchanted chariot, swiftly navigating through the vast expanse of the digital universe.

With this magical tool, people could surf the web, send electronic messages called emails, and uncover a treasure trove of knowledge. It was like having a library, a playground, and a meeting place all rolled into one, accessible from the comfort of your computer.

Bill Gates, the architect of this virtual kingdom, envisioned a future where everyone could be part of the digital revolution. The Internet Age had begun, and it was as if a spell had been cast, connecting people from different corners of the world. Communication became instant, and information flowed like a magical river.

Yet, like any great adventure, challenges arose. In the late 1990s, Microsoft faced legal battles called antitrust issues, questioning its role in shaping the tech industry. But like a resilient hero, Bill Gates continued to lead, undeterred by the storms, and the Internet continued to evolve.

Our journey continues, dear reader, into the next chapters where the landscape of technology shifts, and Bill Gates transitions from leading Microsoft to becoming a benevolent guardian of global well-being. Stay tuned for the magical tale that unfolds in the chapters to come.

Question Time???

When was he born?

When did he start his first business?

Who was his partner?

When did Microsoft start?

Chapter 11
The Antitrust Battle

Alright, young adventurer, buckle up for a chapter filled with twists and turns as we delve into a challenging time for Bill Gates and Microsoft – the Antitrust Battle. Imagine a fierce contest where the rules of the tech kingdom were called into question.

In the late 1990s, Microsoft faced legal challenges over something called "antitrust issues." Now, what's that, you might wonder? Think of it as a referee blowing the whistle during a game to ensure fair play.

In the tech world, it meant making sure that competition among companies was fair and square.

You see, Microsoft had become so powerful that some people felt it wasn't playing by the rules.

It was accused of trying to control too much of the tech landscape, like a giant dragon hoarding all the treasures. This led to a battle in the courts, where lawyers argued over whether Microsoft was being a good player in the tech game.

For Bill Gates, this was a tough time. The company he had built from the ground up was now under scrutiny. But like a hero facing a dragon, Bill continued to lead Microsoft with determination and resilience. Even in the face of challenges, he believed in the importance of Microsoft's mission to make technology accessible to everyone.

Eventually, a settlement was reached. It was like the end of an epic battle, with Microsoft agreeing to play the tech game more fairly. This chapter teaches us that even the mightiest warriors sometimes face challenges, and it's how they respond that defines their character.

Now, as we turn the page to the next chapter, know that our hero, Bill Gates, continues to lead and shape the tech industry. The adventure is far from over, and more exciting tales await. Stay tuned for the next instalment!

Chapter 12

Transition at Microsoft

Hey there, young explorer! We've reached a chapter where our tech hero, Bill Gates, decides to pass on the reins of Microsoft to new leaders. Imagine a relay race, where the baton is handed over to continue the journey. Let's unravel this exciting episode together!

In the year 2000, after years of guiding Microsoft through the tech landscape, Bill Gates made a bold decision. He stepped down as the CEO, which is like the captain of a spaceship handing over control to a skilled crew.

But don't worry, he didn't leave the ship; he just took a different seat on board.

This transition was a significant moment in Microsoft's story.

Bill believed that fresh minds and perspectives were needed to keep the company soaring to new heights. While he might not be steering the ship day-to-day, he remained involved as the company's chief software architect, contributing his wisdom and experience.

Picture it like a seasoned genius passing the magical wand to a new apprentice, ensuring that the magic continues. And indeed, Microsoft continued to cast spells in the tech world under the leadership of others.

But that wasn't the end of Bill's adventures. Instead of being caught up in the day-to-day operations, he shifted his focus to something even more magical - philanthropy. Bill and his then-wife Melinda channelled their energy into the Bill & Melinda Gates Foundation, turning their attention to making the world a better place.

This chapter teaches us an essential lesson - sometimes, change is not only necessary but also a catalyst for new beginnings. Bill Gates continued to shape the tech world in different ways, and his journey evolved into one of

not just creating technology but also using it to make a positive impact on the world.

So, as we move forward in this tale, remember that change can be a powerful force, paving the way for exciting new adventures. The adventure is far from over, and the best is yet to come!

Chapter 13

Gates Foundation Impact

Welcome back, young adventurer! In this chapter, our hero Bill Gates embarks on a mission to make the world a better place using his incredible wealth and knowledge. Let's dive into the extraordinary impact of the Bill & Melinda Gates Foundation.

After accumulating immense success in the tech world, Bill and Melinda Gates decided it was time to share their fortune with the world. In 1994, they founded the Bill & Melinda Gates Foundation, a magical place where dreams of helping people in need came true.

Imagine this foundation as a treasure chest filled with resources dedicated to solving some of the world's most significant challenges. Bill and Melinda set their sights on three major quests: health, education, and tackling poverty.

It was like assembling a superhero team to fight against these global villains.

In the realm of health, Bill Gates became a real-life superhero, using his fortune to fund projects and initiatives to battle diseases that plagued communities worldwide. He targeted enemies like malaria and polio, working tirelessly to make them a thing of the past. The Gates Foundation became a fortress of hope for those in need, spreading magic potions and knowledge to protect lives.

But that's not all! Bill and Melinda extended their reach to the realm of education. They believed that every young mind deserved a chance to grow and learn. Bill even took to the stage with TED Talks, sharing his wisdom about the importance of education and innovation. It was like casting spells of inspiration across the globe, encouraging young minds to dream big.

The Gates Foundation wasn't just about throwing gold coins at problems; it was a place of innovation. Bill continued to support technological advancements,

ensuring that the genius of innovation was used to solve real-world challenges. From improving healthcare systems to addressing global inequalities, the Gates Foundation became a beacon of hope.

As we navigate through this chapter, remember that kindness and generosity can change the world. Bill Gates, once a curious kid tinkering with computers, transformed into a benevolent genius using his magic to create a legacy of compassion and change. So, let the journey continue, for there are still many adventures ahead in the legacy of this visionary!

Chapter 14
Health Initiatives

Hey there, young adventurer! Our hero, Bill Gates, has embarked on a quest to battle invisible foes that threaten the well-being of people around the world. Let's delve into the magical realm of health initiatives and discover how Bill used his powers for good.

Once upon a time, in the late 1990s, Bill Gates shifted his focus to the realm of global health. He envisioned a world where everyone could lead a healthy and fulfilling life.

The Gates Foundation became a fortress against diseases like malaria and polio, where Bill wielded his magic wand to fund initiatives that would make these ailments disappear.

Malaria, a cunning enemy that spreads through

mosquito bites, plagued many lands. Bill, the genius of wellness, poured resources into developing bed nets that acted as shields against these tiny airborne adversaries. The Gates Foundation cast spells to distribute these nets far and wide, protecting vulnerable communities and saving lives.

But that wasn't the only dragon Bill aimed to slay. Polio, a menacing disease affecting the nervous system, had to be vanquished. Our hero sponsored vaccination campaigns across continents, ensuring that children everywhere received the magical elixir that would protect them from this ancient threat. The Gates Foundation worked with knights and healers, forming alliances with organisations worldwide to banish polio from the face of the Earth.

Imagine the Gates Foundation as a magical garden where seeds of health were planted, and the blooms of well-being spread across the world. It wasn't just about treating diseases; it was about preventing them from taking hold in the first place.

Bill's passion for health extended beyond borders. He became a champion for those who didn't have access to the magical potions and treatments they needed. With every initiative, he aimed to create a fair and just world where everyone, regardless of where they lived, could enjoy the benefits of good health.

And so, the tale of Bill Gates, the health genius, continues. As he fought against the forces of sickness, he laid the foundation for a healthier and brighter future for all. Stay tuned for more adventures in the legacy of this visionary!

Chapter 15
TED Talks and Education

Welcome, young minds, to a chapter filled with the magic of ideas and the power of learning! Bill Gates, the genius of wisdom, stepped onto a grand stage called TED Talks to share the secrets of his enchanted journey.

In the world of TED Talks, people gather to listen to great thinkers and visionaries. Bill, armed with his knowledge and passion, took the stage to cast spells of inspiration upon the eager audience.

Picture a spellbinding event where ideas sparkled like stars in the night sky.

Bill spoke of the wonders of technology and the importance of education. He believed that education was the key to unlocking doors to new worlds. With his words,

he enchanted the audience, urging them to embrace the magic of learning and innovation.

The genius Bill emphasised the need for every young adventurer to have access to quality education. He dreamt of a world where knowledge flowed freely, much like a river of wisdom that nurtured the seeds of curiosity in every child. His vision extended beyond the borders of kingdoms, reaching out to those who faced challenges in their quest for learning.

As the TED Talks echoed Bill's vision, the audience became part of a movement—one that celebrated the wonders of knowledge and the joy of discovery. Bill, the storyteller, shared tales of how technology could be a force for good, enhancing the way we learn and connect with one another.

Through his enchanting words, Bill beckoned the youth to become geniuses and smart in their own right, exploring the realms of science, technology, engineering, and mathematics. The magic of innovation, he insisted, could change the world and create a future where

everyone had the opportunity to wield the wand of knowledge.

And so, the TED Talks chapter unfolds, leaving a trail of inspiration and encouraging young minds to dream big, learn passionately, and shape the world with their own magical ideas. Stay tuned for more enchanting adventures in the legacy of this visionary genius!

Chapter 16
Melinda and Bill Foundation

The story of Bill Gates takes an exciting turn as we delve into the chapter where love, partnership, and a shared vision create waves of positive change. Imagine a tale where two hearts, Bill and Melinda, join forces to amplify their impact on the world.

As the Gates Foundation unfolded, Bill and Melinda became a dynamic duo, weaving dreams of a better world. They weren't just adventurers in the realm of technology; they were also knights and sorcerers, using their wealth and wisdom to battle the challenges faced by communities around the globe.

The duo aimed their enchanted weapons of compassion and generosity toward the fields of education and healthcare. Together, they forged alliances with geniuses and

scholars, pooling their resources to cast spells that would improve the lives of countless people.

In the world of education, they sought to break down barriers that kept knowledge locked away from eager minds. They believed that every child, regardless of where they were born, should have the chance to explore the magical realms of learning. The Gates Foundation became a beacon of hope, illuminating the path to quality education for all.

In the realm of healthcare, Bill and Melinda were like healers, concocting potions and antidotes to combat diseases that plagued the lands. They channelled their resources to fight against malaria, polio, and other health foes, aiming to create a world where everyone could thrive in good health.

As the story unfolds, the Gates Foundation becomes a fortress of change, defending against the forces of poverty, inequality, and preventable diseases. Bill and Melinda, with their hearts intertwined, pledged to use their fortune to transform lives and build bridges to a brighter future.

But, dear reader, stay tuned as the tale of Bill Gates continues, for even in the midst of philanthropy, challenges and changes await. The legacy of this visionary duo is far from over, and new chapters of the adventure are yet to be written.

Chapter 17
The Giving Pledge

In this chapter of Bill Gates' incredible journey, we find ourselves in the midst of a grand gathering, where the wealthiest of the wealthy are assembling for a noble cause. The Giving Pledge, initiated by Bill Gates and his friend Warren Buffett in 2010, is an extraordinary event that echoes through the realms of philanthropy.

Picture a majestic hall filled with billionaires from all walks of life, their hearts beating in unison for a shared purpose. The Giving Pledge is like a sacred vow taken by these titans of wealth, promising to dedicate the majority of their fortunes to making the world a better place.

It's not just about acquiring treasures but about sharing the magic of generosity and spreading the wealth of kindness. Bill Gates, with his unwavering belief in the

power of giving, stands before this assembly, urging his fellow billionaires to join the quest. The Giving Pledge is a call to arms, a call to use the power of immense wealth to tackle the great challenges that plague our world – poverty, disease, inequality, and more.

Imagine these billionaires, once rulers of empires built on zeros and ones, now becoming champions of a different kind. They pledge to channel their wealth into the creation of potions that can heal societies, build bridges across deserts of despair, and light the way for those lost in the darkness of poverty.

The Giving Pledge is a commitment to write a new chapter in the history of humanity. It's a story of compassion, where the wealthiest among us decide to rewrite their legacy, not with ink on paper, but with deeds etched in the hearts of those they touch.

As we witness the solemn oaths taken by these billionaires, we sense a shift in the balance of power. It's not just about accumulating more; it's about giving more. Bill Gates, the master storyteller of this saga,

knows that true greatness lies not just in the amassing of wealth but in the selfless act of sharing that wealth for the greater good. And so, the Giving Pledge becomes a beacon of hope, illuminating a path for others to follow in the footsteps of benevolence.

Chapter 18
Technological Innovations

As we delve into the eighteenth chapter of Bill Gates' journey, we find ourselves in a world buzzing with innovation, where ideas are like seeds planted in the fertile soil of progress. Bill, the maestro of technology, has not only shaped the past but is actively influencing the future.

Imagine a landscape filled with brilliant minds working tirelessly in labs and workshops, fueled by a passion for solving the puzzles that perplex humanity. Bill Gates,

having left the helm of Microsoft, now stands on the precipice of the technological frontier, eagerly supporting projects that promise to unravel the mysteries of our ever-evolving world.

This chapter is a tale of futuristic dreams turning into tangible realities. Bill, with the visionary spirit that has always defined him, invests in projects that aim to tackle some of the most pressing issues of our time. Picture a team of scientists working on groundbreaking medical technologies, exploring ways to eradicate diseases that have plagued humanity for centuries. Bill Gates, the benefactor of progress, is there, guiding them with his unwavering belief in the power of innovation.

Technology, under Bill's watchful eye, becomes a tool not just for convenience but for creating a better world. The stage is set for inventions that could change the course of history – from advanced medical treatments to sustainable energy solutions, the possibilities are limitless.

In this chapter, we witness the birth of ideas that transcend the ordinary, ideas that have the potential to touch the lives of people across the globe. Bill Gates, ever the pioneer, understands that the true power of technology lies not just in its ability to entertain or make tasks easier but in its potential to transform lives, uplift communities, and bridge gaps.

As we navigate through the wonders of technological innovation in this chapter, we see a glimpse of a future where problems are not obstacles but opportunities for creative minds to shine. Bill Gates, the guide through this realm of discovery, continues to leave an indelible mark on the landscape of progress, ensuring that technology becomes a force for good, a beacon of hope in the ever-expanding universe of human achievement.

Chapter 19
Personal Life and Changes

As we open the pages of Chapter 19, we step into the more personal side of Bill Gates' extraordinary journey. It's a chapter that explores the twists and turns life takes, even for someone as accomplished as Bill.

In 2021, the headlines echoed with news about Bill and Melinda Gates, a couple who had stood side by side in both their personal and philanthropic endeavors for many years.

They announced a significant change - a decision to go separate ways in their personal lives. It's a moment where we see that even the most successful individuals face challenges and changes.

Just like in a great novel, life's narrative isn't always predictable.

Bill and Melinda, who together had shaped the course of technology and philanthropy, found themselves at a crossroads. But, in the face of personal changes, they made a unique commitment. Instead of letting this divergence mark the end, they pledged to continue their collaborative efforts through the Gates Foundation.

This chapter is a glimpse into the resilience of the human spirit, even when faced with the unexpected. It speaks to the idea that, no matter how meticulously one plans, life remains an unpredictable adventure. The divorce announcement doesn't mark the end of their shared journey; rather, it symbolises a new chapter where their dedication to making a positive impact on the world persists.

For young readers, this chapter holds a valuable lesson - that change is a constant in life. And, just as Bill Gates adapted to the ever-evolving world of technology, he also adapted to the changes in his personal life. It's a reminder that challenges are a part of everyone's story, but how we navigate them and the choices we make define our character.

As we turn the pages, we are left with a sense of anticipation. What will the next chapter bring for Bill Gates, for Melinda, and for the causes they hold dear? The legacy of a visionary is not just in the accomplishments but in the ability to face change with courage and continue the journey, knowing that the story is far from over.

Chapter 20
Legacy of a Visionary

As we delve into the final chapter of Bill Gates' remarkable journey, we witness the legacy of a visionary unfolding before us. Bill's story isn't just about the creation of technology; it's about the lasting impact one person can have on the world.

LEGACY

Today, Bill Gates stands as a beacon, not only in the tech industry but as a dedicated philanthropist. His legacy goes beyond the codes and programs he wrote; it extends to the lives he touched and the positive changes he brought about.

The first pages of this chapter reveal that Bill's influence stretches far beyond the boardrooms of Microsoft. He's a pioneer who dedicated himself to making a difference in global health and education. The computer screens that once displayed lines of code now reflect his commitment to solving some of the world's most pressing issues.

Bill's passion for technology and innovation didn't end with his role at Microsoft. Instead, he redirected his focus toward philanthropy, channelling his wealth and influence to address challenges that affect millions. Through the Bill & Melinda Gates Foundation, he continued to tackle issues like poverty, disease, and lack of access to education.

For you, this chapter serves as an inspiration. It teaches that success isn't just measured by personal achievements but by the positive impact one can have on the lives of others. Bill Gates exemplifies the idea that success is a journey with many chapters, each offering an opportunity to contribute to the greater good.

The Giving Pledge, initiated by Bill Gates and Warren Buffett, invites billionaires to commit the majority of their wealth to philanthropy. This is a crucial part of Bill's legacy – inspiring others to join the mission of making the world a better place.

As we reach the final paragraphs of this chapter, we see that the legacy of a visionary isn't just about the past; it's about the future. Bill Gates, with his vision and actions, has set the stage for a world where technology and compassion work hand in hand. The last lines invite us to ponder what contributions young minds can make to shape a future where innovation and kindness coexist.

And so, the story of Bill Gates, the curious kid who became a billionaire and a philanthropist, closes with the realisation that the impact of a visionary isn't confined to a single lifetime. It echoes in the hearts of those inspired to dream big, create, and give back to the world.

Question Time???

When did he step down as the CEO of Microsoft?

What is the name of the stage where he shared the secret of his enchanted journey?

What is the name of the philanthropic foundation he started with his wife?

What do you love about him?

Facts About Bill Gates

Facts About Bill Gates

His full name is William Henry Gates III.

Gates co-founded Microsoft in 1975 with Paul Allen.

He dropped out of Harvard University to pursue his passion for computer programming and entrepreneurship.

Gates' first computer program was a tic-tac-toe game at the age of 13.

Facts About Bill Gates

BASIC, a popular programming language, was one of the first software products created by Gates.

Microsoft's big break came when they signed a deal with IBM to provide an operating system for their first personal computer.

Windows 1.0 was released in 1985 as Microsoft's first graphical user interface.

The Gates Foundation focuses on global health, education, and poverty alleviation.

Facts About Bill Gates

Bill Gates is a voracious reader, known to read about 50 books a year.

He owns a rare copy of Leonardo da Vinci's notebook, which he bought for over $30 million.

Gates has been the world's richest person for several years, although his position fluctuates due to market changes.

He is an avid bridge player and competed at a high level.

Facts About Bill Gates

He received an honorary knighthood from Queen Elizabeth II in 2005.

Gates and Paul Allen were childhood friends and attended Lakeside School together.

The first computer program Gates created was a payroll system for his school.

Gates has invested in various ventures outside of Microsoft, including Corbis, a digital image licensing and rights services company.

Facts About Bill Gates

He is known for his love of hamburgers, and his favorite fast-food chain is reported to be Dick's Drive-In in Seattle.

He received the Presidential Medal of Freedom in 2016 from President Barack Obama.

Gates and Paul Allen were inspired by the first commercially available microcomputer, the Altair 8800, to start Microsoft.

Gates was a guest lecturer at Stanford University, where he delivered the "How to Start a Startup" series.

Life Lessons from Bill Gates

Life Lessons from Bill Gates

Gates faced failures early in his career but used them as learning opportunities to ultimately achieve success.

Gates is a voracious reader, emphasizing the importance of ongoing learning throughout life.

Gates took the risk of starting Microsoft with Paul Allen, a decision that ultimately changed the technolog landscape.

Microsoft evolved from a software company to a tech giant, showcasing the importance of adapting to changing markets.

Life Lessons from Bill Gates

Gates is known for his intense work ethic and dedication to Microsoft's success.

Gates and his ex-wife Melinda founded the Bill & Melinda Gates Foundation, demonstrating the importance of philanthropy.

Gates has been an advocate for global health initiatives, emphasizing the importance of well-being.

Despite his success, Gates remains humble and open to learning from others.

Bill Gates

www.ingramcontent.com/pod-product-compliance
Ingram Content Group UK Ltd.
Pitfield, Milton Keynes, MK11 3LW, UK
UKHW050626170225
4621UKWH00054B/684

9 785736 918485